Bo

A dog journal for you to record your dog's life as it happens!

Copyright © 2013
By Debbie Miller

This book is © copyrighted by the author Debbie Miller and is protected under the US Copyright Act of 1976 and all other applicable international, federal, state and local laws, with ALL rights reserved.

This book contains protected material. No part of this may be copied, or changed in any format, sold, or used in any way. Any unauthorized reprint or use of this material is prohibited, including photocopying, recording, or by any information storage and retrieval system without written permission from the author/publisher.

Introduction

This Border Collie journal preserves the precious moments!

There is lots of space for snapshots of your best friend and companion! This blank book gives dog lovers the opportunity to chart their puppies growth.

As your puppy grows into an adult you can document and capture the cherished moments.

There is a page for birth information, vaccine records, and even a page to place your puppy's paw prints!

You can take photos of your puppy discovering his world as he grows into an adult. This blank book is the ultimate keepsake for every dog owner!

There are pages that allow you to add a photo then write what your puppy or dog did that day.

Don't miss the happy moments when your companion is sleeping, bounding across the yard, his first birthday or his favorite things to do!

With this dog memory book you will be able to admire and preserve your favorite memories to enjoy the happy moments for years!

Start creating lasting memories today with this journal and scrapbook for your puppy or dog!

*A dog is the only thing on earth that loves
you more than you love yourself.
~Josh Billings*

*A dog will teach you unconditional love.
If you can have that in your life, things won't be too bad.
~Robert Wagner*

My Border Collie

Date of Birth: _____

Place of Birth: _____

Registered Name: _____

Call Name: _____

Father's Name: _____

Mother's Name: _____

Puppy Paw Print

Adult Paw Print

Vaccination Records

Age	Shot Date	Distemper	Parvo	Rabies	Deworm
6 wks					
10 wks					
14 wks					
1 Year					
2 Year					
3 Year					
4 Year					
5 Year					
6 Year					
7 Year					
8 Year					
9 Year					
10 Year					
11 Year					
12 Year					

Additional Medical:

Heartworm Testing:

1 Year___ 2 Year___ 3 Year ___ 4 Year___ 5 Year___

6 Year___ 7 Year___ 8 Year ___ 9 Year___ 10 Year___

Vaccination Notes:

_____

_____

Medical Record Notes:

Medical Emergencies

Memories

Don't miss the happy moments!

Start creating lasting memories today!

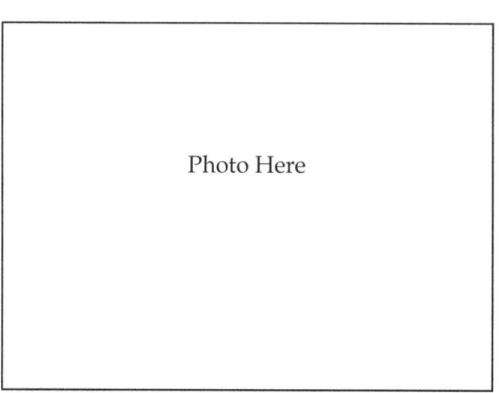

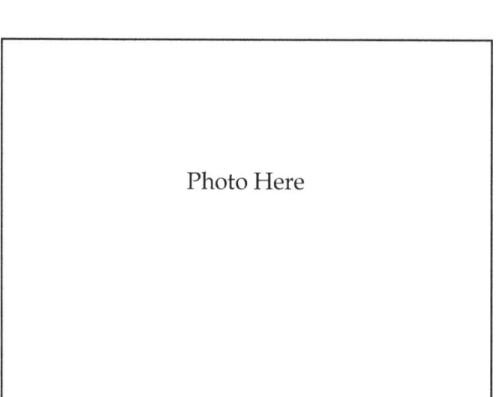

Memories:

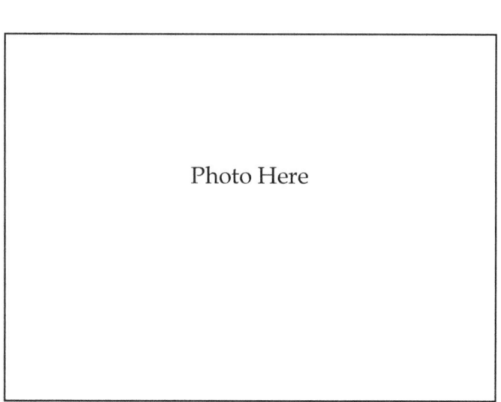

Memories:

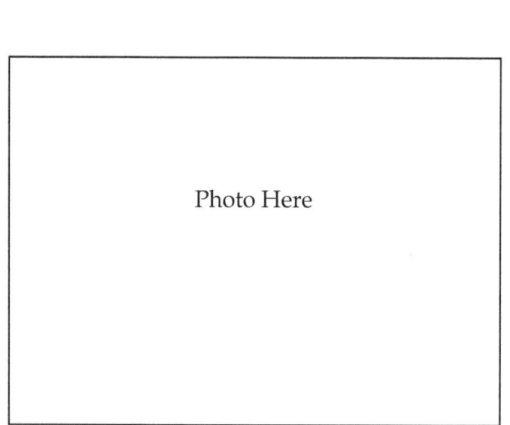

Memories:

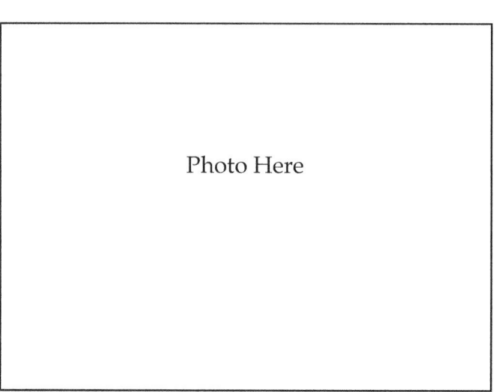

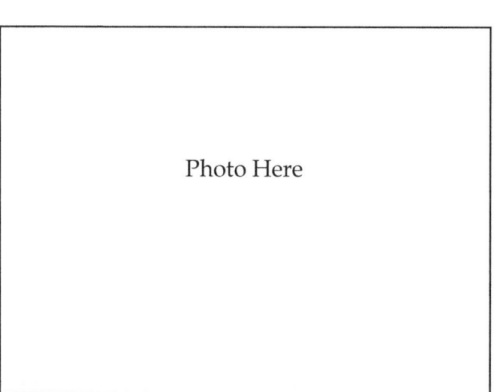

Memories:

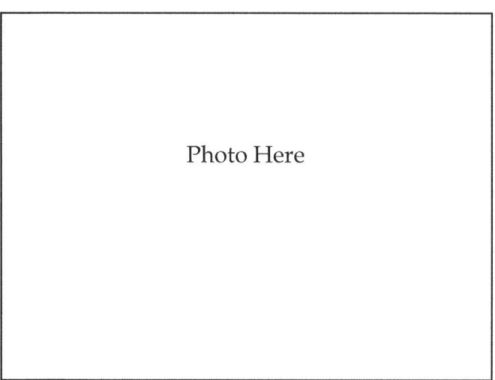

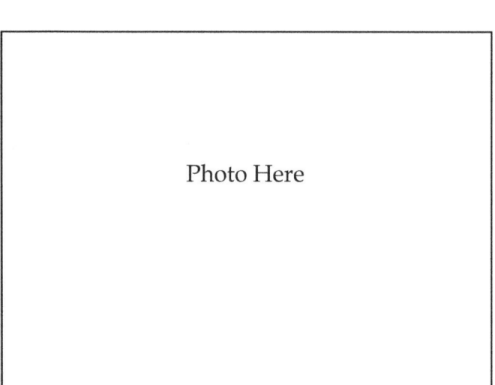

Memories:

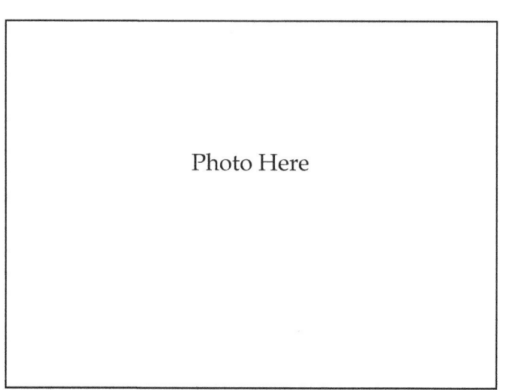

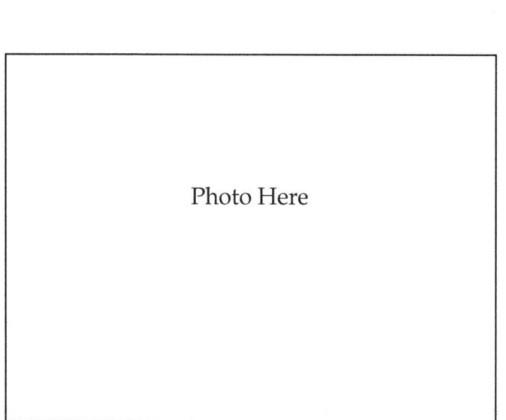

Memories:

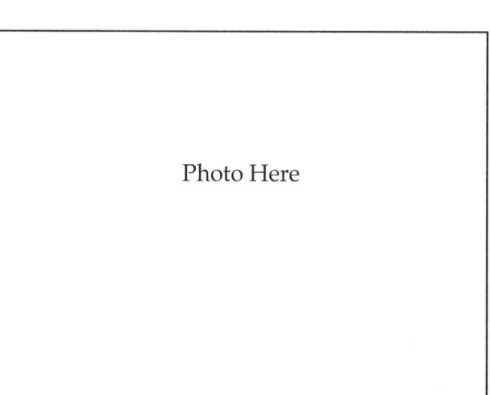

Memories:

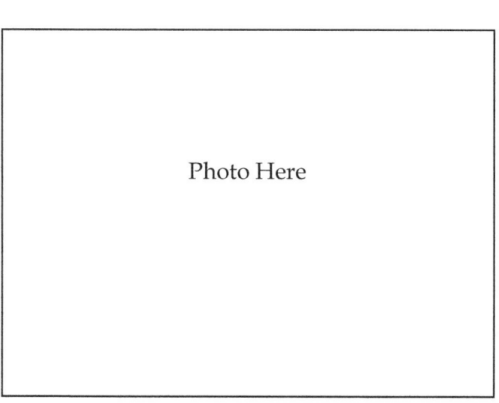

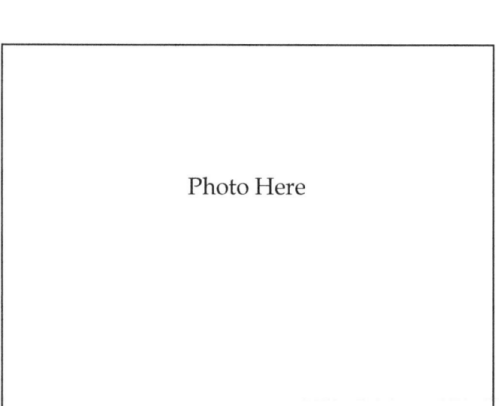

Memories:

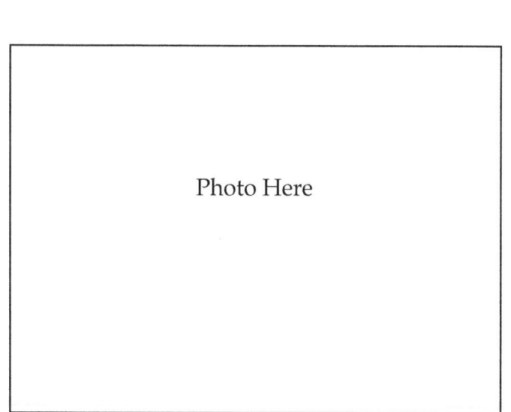

Memories:

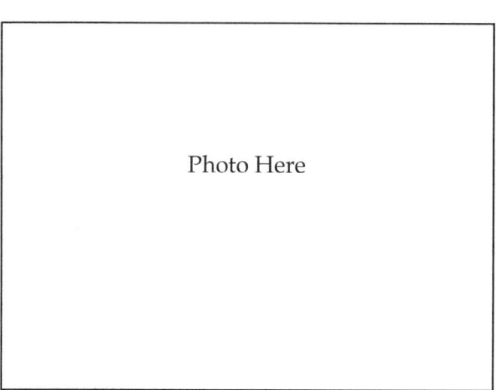

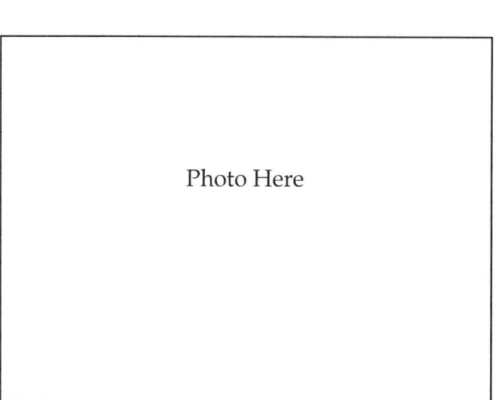

Memories:

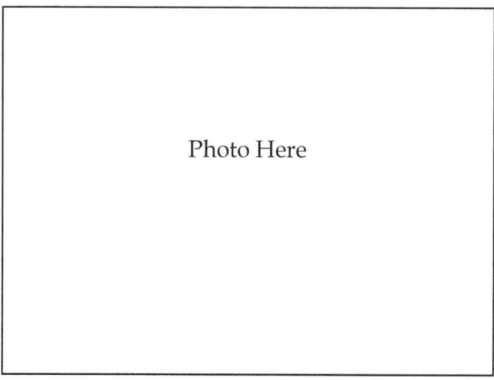

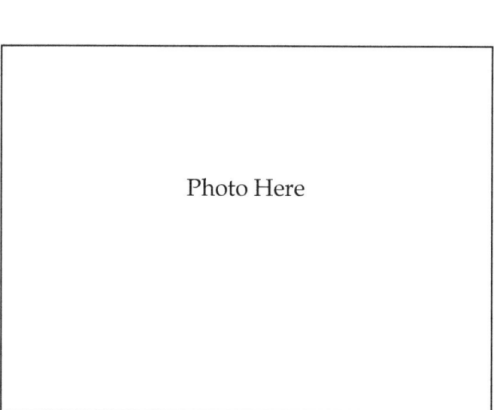

Memories:

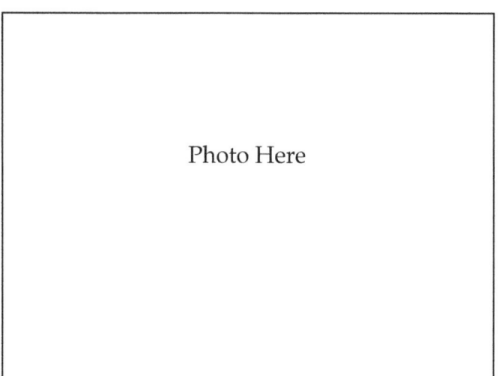

Memories:

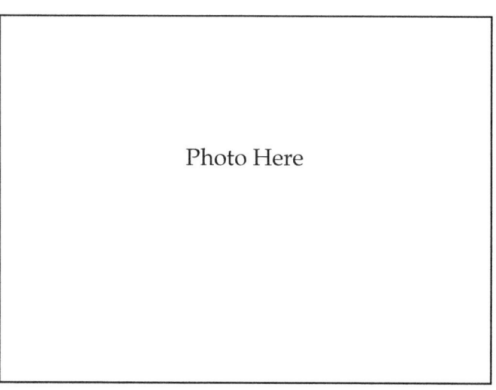

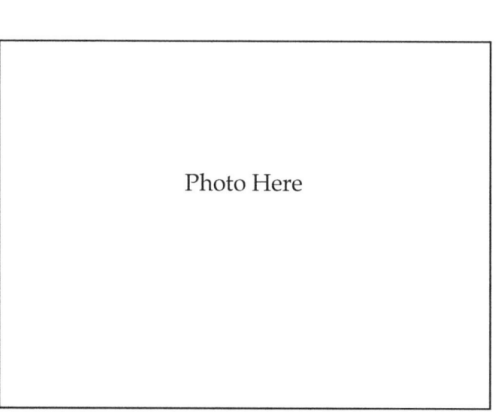

Memories:

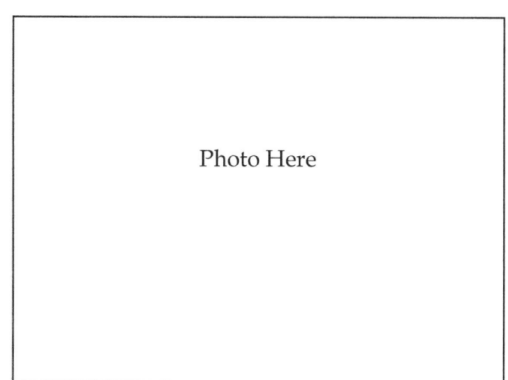

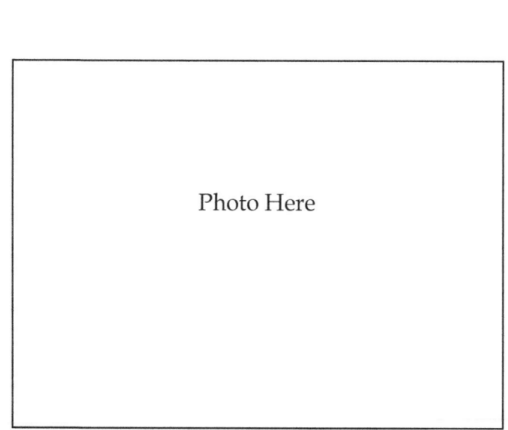

Memories:

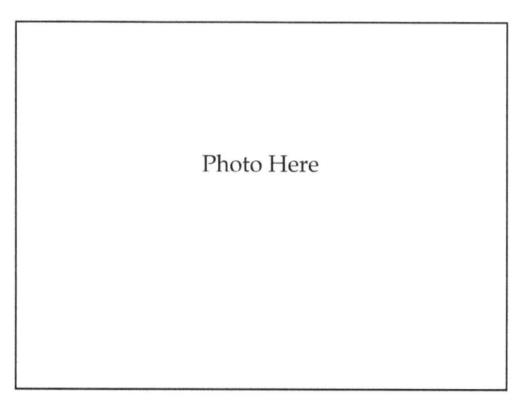

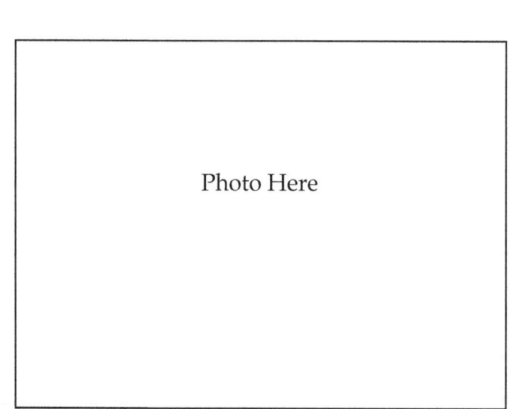

Memories:

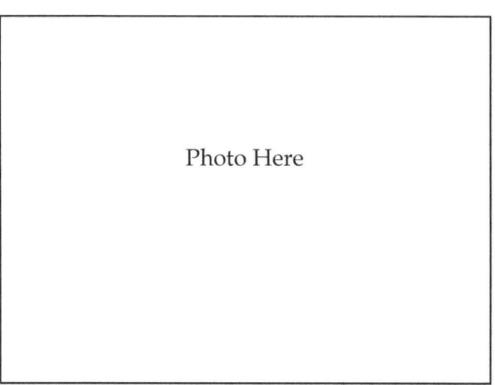

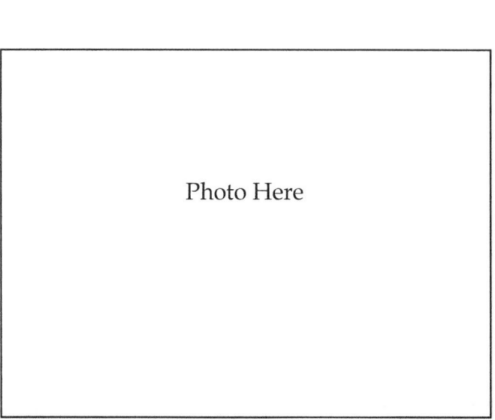

Memories:

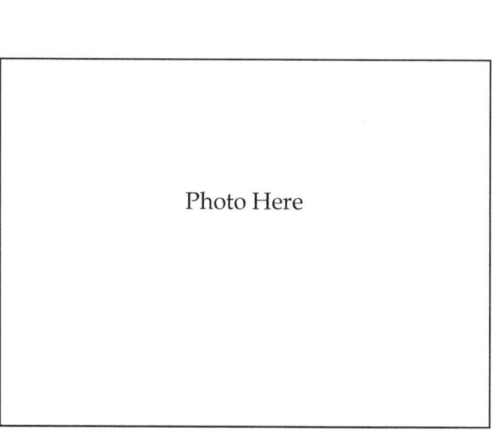

Memories:

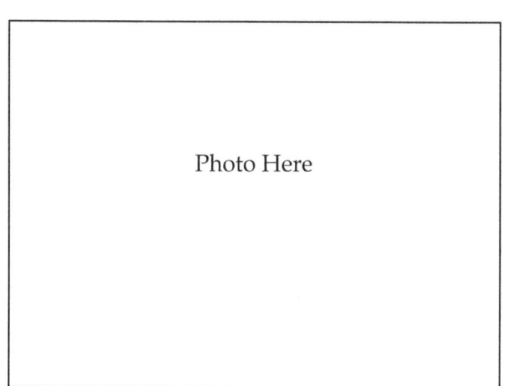

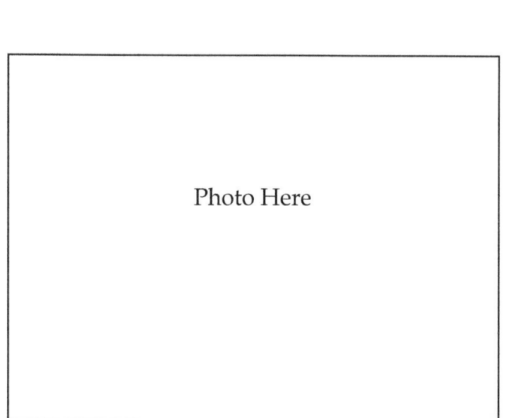

Memories:

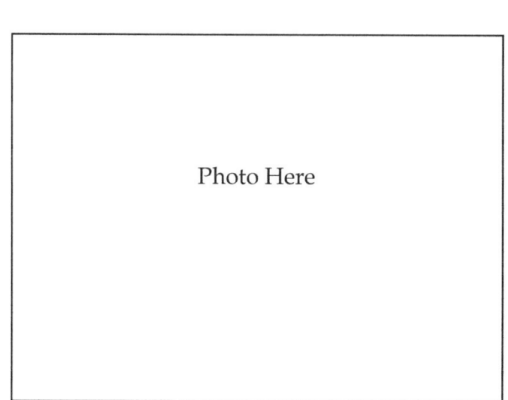

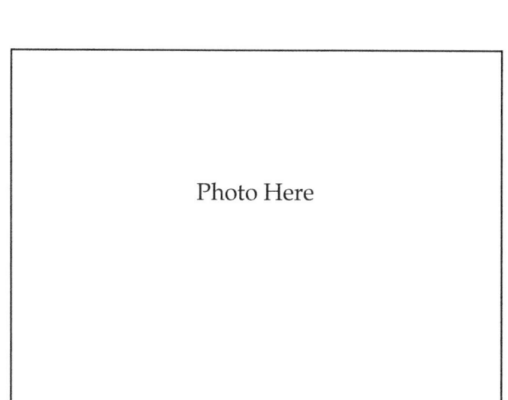

Memories:

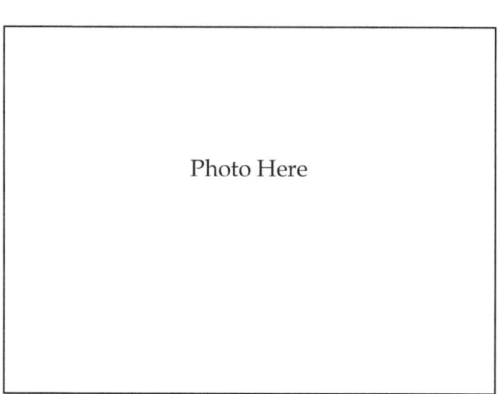

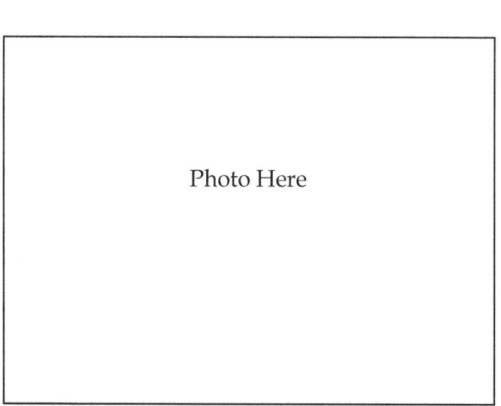

Memories:

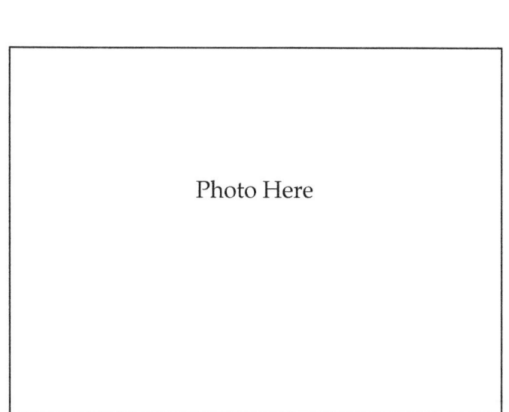

Memories:

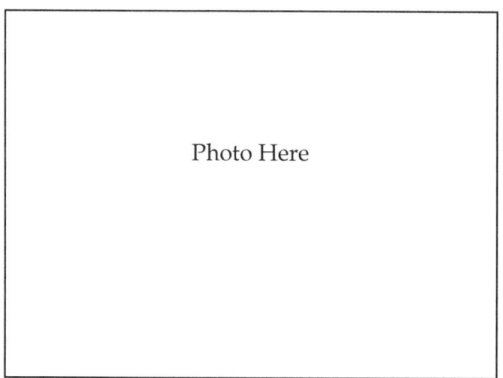

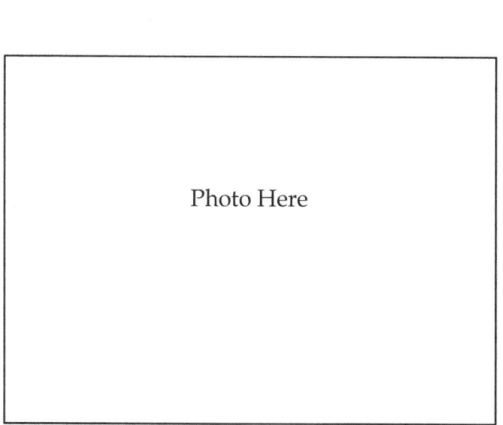

Memories:

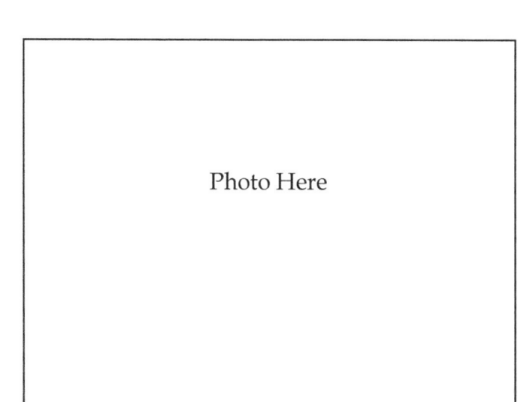

Memories:

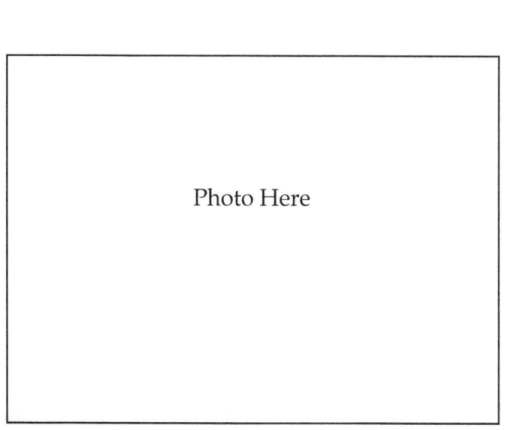

Memories:

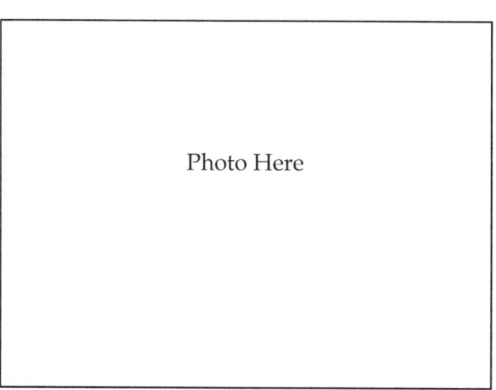

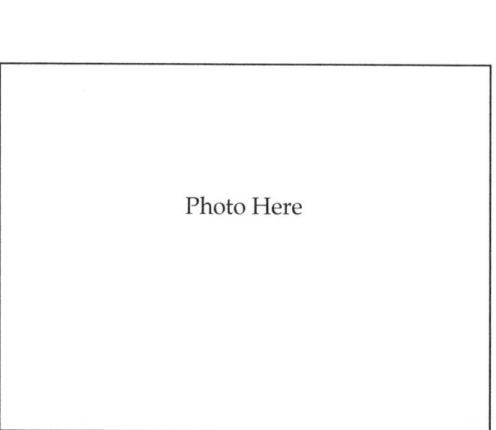

Memories:

CPSIA information can be obtained at www.ICGtesting.com
Printed in the USA
LVOW04s2042101014

408240LV00015B/255/P

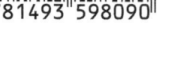